Events of
1939

News for every day of the year

Civil Defence exercise,
Fulham, west London.

By Hugh Morrison

MONTPELIER PUBLISHING
LONDON

Published in Great Britain by Montpelier Publishing, London.

Distributed by Amazon Createspace/KDP.

January 1939

Sunday 1: Information technology company Hewlett-Packard is founded in a garage in Palo Alto, California.

Monday 2: The highest ever attendance at an association football match (118,567) is seen at Ibrox Park in Glasgow when Rangers beat Celtic.

Tuesday 3: In the Spanish Civil War, nationalist forces are victorious in the Battle of the Segre.

Wednesday 4: US President Franklin D. Roosevelt gives his State of the Union address to Congress, in which he warns that 'peace is not assured.'

F.D. Roosevelt.

Thursday 5: During discussions with the Polish Foreign Minister Jozef Beck, Adolf Hitler demands that the Free City of Danzig be returned to Germany.

Friday 6: Notorious gangster Al Capone is transferred from Alcatraz to Terminal Island jail to serve the last year of his sentence.

Jozef Beck.

Saturday 7: The German battleship *Scharnhorst* is commissioned.

Sunday 8: Charles Eastman (also known by his tribal name of 'Hakada'), American Indian doctor and reformer, dies aged 80.

Left: Al Capone.

January 1939

Neville Chamberlain, Prime Minister of Great Britain.

Monday 9: A new Reich Chancellery designed by Albert Speer is inaugurated in Berlin.

Tuesday 10: Britain's Prime Minister Neville Chamberlain and foreign minister Lord Halifax pledge support to France in the event of any Italian attacks on French colonies.

Wednesday 11: Neville Chamberlain and Lord Halifax meet Benito Mussolini in Rome, hoping to persuade him to advise Hitler against war.

Thursday 12: Country singer William Lee Golden of the Oak Ridge Boys is born in Brewton, Alabama.

Friday 13: The horror film *Son of Frankenstein* starring Basil Rathbone and Boris Karloff is released.

Saturday 14: Adolf Hitler adopts the sole title 'Führer' (leader).

Sunday 15: US talk show host Maury Povich is born in Washington, DC.

Berlin's new Reich Chancellery, designed by architect Albert Speer. The vast building was largely destroyed by Allied action in 1945.

January 1939

Monday 16: Five bombs explode in London and three in Manchester, as the Irish Republican Army (IRA) begins a mainland bombing campaign.

Adolf Hitler.

Tuesday 17: Following further IRA bomb attacks in Manchester, London and Birmingham, all power stations, gas works and telephone exchanges are put under police protection.

Wednesday 18: Police arrest 14 IRA suspects and step up inspections of all shipping arriving from Ireland.

Thursday 19: Philip Everly of the Everly Brothers born in Chicago, Illinois (died 2014).

Friday 20: Nationalist forces capture Calaf in Catalonia, Spain.

Saturday 21: Adolf Hitler orders the government of Czechoslovakia to quit the League of Nations and to pass antisemitic legislation.

Sunday 22: The cargo ship SS *Wilston* runs aground near Land's End, Cornwall, England, with the loss of all 30 crew.

Phil Everly (left), born 19 January 1939.

January 1939

Civil Defence volunteer co-ordinator, Fulham, London.

Monday 23: Prime Minister Neville Chamberlain launches a recruitment drive for Britain's Civil Defence Corps, volunteers trained for emergency service in the event of air raids or invasion.

Tuesday 24: The adventure film *Gunga Din* starring Cary Grant and Douglas Fairbanks Jr premieres in Los Angeles.

Wednesday 25: Joe Louis retains the world heavyweight boxing title when he knocks down opponent John Henry Lewis three times at Madison Square Garden, New York.

Thursday 26: Filming begins on the epic romance film *Gone with the Wind* starring Vivien Leigh and Clark Gable.

Friday 27: Adolf Hitler approves 'Plan Z', the construction of 800 ships for the German navy by 1948.

Saturday 28: Nationalist forces begin air raids on Barcelona, Spain.

Sunday 29: Feminist author Germaine Greer is born.

Cinema poster for *Gunga Din*.

January/February 1939

Monday 30: Hitler warns that if 'Jewish financiers' start a war, it will lead to the 'annhilation of the Jewish race in Europe'.

Tuesday 31: US President Roosevelt announces 'if the Rhine frontiers are threatened, the rest of the world is, too.' This is widely interpreted by the US press as being pro-interventionist.

Wednesday 1: The Soviet Union closes its embassy in Budapest in protest at Hungary's decision to join the pro-German Anti Comintern Pact.

Thursday 2: Spanish Republican forces ask Britain and France for aid in negotiating a ceasefire with nationalists.

Friday 3: The musical film *Honolulu*, starring Eleanor Powell and Robert Young is released.

Saturday 4: Seven people are injured in London when IRA bombs explode at Tottenham Court Road and Leicester Square underground stations.

Sunday 5: Nationalist troops take Girona in the Catalonia Offensive in Spain.

Volunteer Republican (anti-Francoist) fighters in Spain.

February 1939

Pope Pius XI.

Monday 6: Britain's Prime Minister Neville Chamberlain is applauded in the House of Commons when he states that any attack by Germany upon France will result in British retaliation.

Tuesday 7: In the Spanish Civil War, the Battle of Minorca begins, ending two days later in a Republican defeat.

Wednesday 8: Nationalist forces capture Figueres in Spain.

Thursday 9: The British government announces plans to distribute pre-fabricated air raid shelters (Anderson Shelters) to thousands of homes in districts thought to be at risk from air raids.

Anderson Shelter.

Friday 10: Pope Pius XI dies aged 81.

Saturday 11: Pilot Benjamin S. Kelsey sets a world speed record in a prototype Lockheed P-38 Lightning fighter plane, flying from California to New York in just over seven hours.

Sunday 12: Over 200,000 people arrive in Rome for the Pope's funeral.

February 1939

Monday 13: In Spain, General Franco decrees that all persons hostile to the nationalist cause will lose their citizenship and be exiled.

Tuesday 14: The German battleship *Bismarck* is launched.

Wednesday 15: John Ford's western film *Stagecoach*, featuring John Wayne in his first major acting role, is released.

George Bancroft, John Wayne and Louise Platt in *Stagecoach*.

Thursday 16: Pál Teleki replaces Béla Imrédy as prime minister of Hungary, after it is revealed that Imrédy, who pursued anti-semitic policies, has Jewish ancestry.

Friday 17: Adolf Hitler opens the Berlin Motor Show, which includes the new Volkswagen car, later known as the Beetle or Bug.

Saturday 18: The Golden Gate International Exposition opens in San Francisco, California.

Sunday 19: An unsuccessful attempt is made by army officers to overthrow the government of Peru while while President Óscar R. Benavides is away on holiday.

February 1939

Monday 20: Violent clashes take place in New York between pro- and anti-nazi demonstrators.

Tuesday 21: Persecution of Jews in Nazi Germany intensifies, with a decree that all Jews are to turn in their gold, silver and other valuables to the state without compensation.

Wednesday 22: The British government authorises aircraft production to reach maximum levels regardless of cost.

Thursday 23: The first pay-per-view sporting event takes place in London's Harringay Arena as three cinemas show a live televised boxing match between Eric Boon and Arthur Danahar.

Friday 24: Hungary joins the Anti-Comintern pact in opposition to Soviet communism.

Saturday 25: German authorities begin giving notice to all Jews to leave the country within two weeks.

Sunday 26: Around 1000 people attend a demonstration in London opposing Britain's recognition of the Franco regime in Spain.

Nazis boycott Jewish businesses in Berlin.

February/March 1939

The first US edition of *Mein Kampf*.

Monday 27: Britain and France formally recognise Francoist Spain.

Tuesday 28: Two editions of Hitler's autobiography, *Mein Kampf*, are published by rival firms on the same day in the USA, with one of the firms, Stackpole and Sons, proudly advertising that Hitler will receive no royalties and all profits will go to refugees.

Wednesday 1: The Papal Conclave meets in the Vatican to appoint a new pope.

Thursday 2: The new pope, Pius XII *(right)* is announced. Although the Vatican is officially neutral, he maintains links to the German resistance against Hitler.

Friday 3: Mahatma Gandhi begins a fast over political reforms in Rajkot, India.

Saturday 4: The Cartagena Uprising begins in Spain as the Republican fifth columnists fight back against occupying nationalists in the city.

Sunday 5: Actress Samantha Eggar *(right)* (*The Collector, Dr Doolittle, All My Children*) is born in London, England.

March 1939

Monday 6: The Infanta Margarita of Spain, aunt of the present king HM Felipe VI, is born in Rome.

Tuesday 7: Mahatma Gandhi ends his four day fast and accepts an invitation from the Viceroy of India to attend a political conference in Delhi.

Wednesday 8: General Franco declares a total blockade of all Republican held ports in Spain.

Thursday 9: US-Brazilian Agreements: the United States agrees to send financial assistance and economic development aid to Brazil.

General Franco.

Mahatma Gandhi.

Friday 10: 20 members of the IRA are sentenced to life imprisonment for their parts in the campaign to bomb mainland Britain earlier in the year.

Saturday 11: A new pro-German cabinet is formed in autonomous Slovakia after a virtual coup d'etat by neighbouring Czechoslovakia.

Sunday 12: Pope Pius XII is crowned. He is the first native Roman to hold the office since 1731.

March 1939

Emil Hácha meets Hitler in Berlin.

Monday 13: Singer and pianist Neil Sedaka is born in Brooklyn, New York.

Tuesday 14: The trial begins of the Philadelphia Poison Ring, a gang of Italian-American contract killers who had been operating since 1930.

Wednesday 15: Adolf Hitler meets with Emil Hácha, the Czechoslovakian president, in Berlin and offers him the choice of a peaceable takeover of the country or total destruction. Faced with overwhelming military superiority, Hácha capitulates.

Thursday 16: Czechoslovakia officially ceases to exist and is divided into the states of Slovakia, the Sudetenland and the Protectorate of Bohemia and Moravia.

Friday 17: Prime Minister Neville Chamberlain condemns Germany's breaking of its territorial agreements made at Munich in 1938, and states that Britain will oppose any further German expansion.

Saturday 18: James Thurber's short story *The Secret Life of Walter Mitty* is first published, in the *New Yorker* magazine.

Sunday 19: Egyptologist Pierre Montet announces the finding of the tomb of Psusennes I near Port Said, Egypt.

The death mask of the pharoah Psusennes I, discovered by Pierre Montet.

March 1939

Monday 20: Germany issues an ultimatum to Lithuania demanding control of its Klaipėda Region.

Tuesday 21: Lithuania capitulates to Germany and hands over the territory of Klaipėda.

Wednesday 22: Hermann Petrillo, leader of the Philadelphia Poison Ring, is sentenced to death for his role in multiple homicides.

Thursday 23: Soldiers of the Hungarian army, allied to Germany, march into Slovakia to reclaim territory that was taken from Hungary at the Treaty of Trianon (Versailles) in 1920.

Friday 24: The film adaptation of Emily Bronte's novel *Wuthering Heights* is released, starring Merle Oberon and Laurence Olivier.

Saturday 25: Italy issues an ultimatum to Albania, demanding it be established as an Italian protectorate.

Sunday 26: A large oil field is discovered at Eakring, Nottinghamshire, which goes on to produce 3.5 million barrels of oil during the Second World War.

Laurence Olivier and Merle Oberon in *Wuthering Heights*.

March/April 1939

Monday 27: Francoist Spain joins the Anti-Comintern Pact.

Tuesday 28: The three year long Siege of Madrid ends as Nationalist forces capture the city.

Wednesday 29: Britain announces plans to double the size of its Territorial Army (volunteer reserve forces).

Thursday 30: Cartoon superhero Batman makes his first appearance in *Detective Comics* issue number 27.

SAFEGUARD YOUR LIBERTIES!

JOIN THE TERRITORIAL ARMY

Recruitment poster for Britain's reserve forces

Friday 31: The British and French governments pledge support for Poland if it is invaded by Germany.

Saturday 1: General Franco announces the victory of Nationalist forces in the Spanish Civil War.

Sunday 2: Singer and songwriter Marvin Gaye is born in Washington, DC (died 1984).

Street fighting in the Siege of Madrid.

April 1939

Monday 3: Hitler approves top secret plans for the German invasion of Poland from 1 September onwards.

Glenn Miller.

Tuesday 4: Glenn Miller and his Orchestra record their hit tune *Moonlight Serenade.*

Wednesday 5: Britain's largest aircraft carrier, HMS *Illustrious,* is launched at Barrow-in-Furness.

Thursday 6: Albania rejects Italy's demands for it to become a protectorate.

Friday 7: Italy invades Albania; Albanian forces provide only token resistance.

Marian Anderson in concert.

Saturday 8: King Zog of Albania flees to neighbouring Greece.

Sunday 9: Easter Sunday: black singer Marian Anderson gives an outdoor concert in front of c.75,000 in Washington DC after being refused permission to perform in the racially segregated DAR Constitution Hall.'

April 1939

Marty Wilde.

Monday 10: Germany begins to station troops on the border with the Netherlands.

Tuesday 11: Hungary announces its withdrawal from the League of Nations.

Wednesday 12: Prolific English playwright Alan Ayckbourn (*Season's Greetings, Bedroom Farce*) is born in Hampstead, London.

Thursday 13: Poet Seamus Heaney is born in Castledawson, County Londonderry (died 2013).

Friday 14: John Steinbeck's 'dustbowl' novel *The Grapes of Wrath* is published.

Dusty Springfield.

John Steinbeck.

Saturday 15: Singer Marty Wilde MBE (*A Teenager in Love*), father of 80s singer Kim Wilde, is born in London.

Sunday 16: Singer Dusty Springfield is born in West Hampstead, London (died 1999).

April 1939

Monday 17: Joe Louis retains the world heavyweight boxing title by knocking out Jack Roper in the first round at Wrigley Field, Los Angeles.

Billie Holiday.

Tuesday 18: The British government pledges assistance to the Netherlands, Denmark and Switzerland if attacked.

Wednesday 19: Ellison Brown wins the Boston Marathon with a time of 2.28:51.

The San Jacinto Monument.

Thursday 20: Billie Holiday records anti-lynching blues song *Strange Fruit*.

Friday 21: The San Jacinto Monument, commemorating the centenary of the victory of Texan forces over Mexico in 1839, is dedicated at Harris County, Texas.

Saturday 22: The film *Dark Victory*, starring Bette Davis and Humphrey Bogart, is released.

Sunday 23: Actor Lee Majors (*The Six Million Dollar Man*) is born in Wyandotte, Michigan.

April 1939

Monday 24: Germán Busch, President of Bolivia, announces the dissolution of the country's national assembly and assumes dictatorial powers.

Tuesday 25: Britain's Chancellor of the Exchequer announces tax increases to fund the country's increasing defence budget.

Wednesday 26: Robert Menzies becomes the 12th Prime Minister of Australia.

Robert Menzies, PM of Australia.

Thursday 27: The British government announces the introduction of military conscription for all men aged 20 to 21.

Friday 28: Hitler revokes prior German agreements on limiting the size of its navy, and renounces the German-Polish Non-Agression Pact of 1934.

Saturday 29: Portsmouth beats Wolverhampton Wanderers 4-1 in the last Football Association (FA) Cup Final to be held before 1946.

Sunday 30: The 1939 New York World's Fair is opened by President Roosevelt; the first NBC television broadcast is coverage of the event.

Ford Motors pavilion, New York World's Fair.

May 1939

Monday 1: During May Day celebrations, Hitler warns Germans that they must 'unite or perish'.

Tuesday 2: 30,000 Jews are stripped of their citizenship in Slovakia.

Wednesday 3: A Gallup poll reports that 84 per cent of Americans are opposed to US involvement in a European war.

Dorothy Garrod, the first female professor at Cambridge.

Thursday 4: James Joyce's 'experimental' novel *Finnegan's Wake* is published.

Friday 5: Archaeologist Dorothy Garrod becomes the first female professor at Cambridge University.

Saturday 6: The Kentucky Derby is won by 'Johnstown' ridden by James Stout.

Sunday 7: Italy and Germany announce their intention of forming a military alliance.

Jockey James Stout, here seen with his wife Eileen, rides 'Johnstown' to victory in the Kentucky Derby.

May 1939

Monday 8: Britain offers to mediate in the German-Polish dispute over territorial rights in the city of Danzig (Gdansk).

Mongolian troops at Khalkyn Gol.

Tuesday 9: Japanese forces are victorious in the Battle of Nanchang, part of the Second Sino-Japanese War.

Wednesday 10: Henry Miller's autobiographical novel *Tropic of Capricorn* is published in France. It is banned in the USA on grounds of obscenity until 1961.

Thursday 11: Russian and Mongolian troops clash with invading Japanese forces at the Battle of Khalkyn Gol on the Chinese border.

Friday 12: Britain and Turkey announce a mutual aid agreement in the event of war. The treaty has no practical value as Turkey does not declare war on Germany until February 1945.

Saturday 13: Actor Harvey Keitel *(right)* (*Reservoir Dogs, Cop Land*) is born in Brooklyn, New York.

Sunday 14: Peruvian Lina Medina, aged five, becomes the youngest woman on record to give birth, after developing a condition causing extreme early onset of puberty. The child, a healthy boy, lives until the age of 40. Miss Medina never reveals the identity of the child's father.

May 1939

Monday 15: School drama film *Goodbye Mr Chips*, starring Robert Donat and Greer Garson, premieres in London.

Tuesday 16: The Food Stamps welfare programme begins in the USA.

Wednesday 17: TM King George VI and Queen Elizabeth begin a royal tour of Canada; the King is the first British sovereign to visit Canada.

Thursday 18: Jews riot in Jerusalem following the announcement of plans to limit Jewish immigration into British Palestine.

Friday 19: Actor James Fox (*The Servant, Performance*) is born in London.

Saturday 20: Pan-American airways begins a regular airmail service between the USA and Europe.

Sunday 21: HM King George VI dedicates Canada's National War Memorial in Ottawa.

Their Majesties the King and Queen of Canada on the Royal Train.

May 1939

USS *Squalus.*

Monday 22: Germany and Italy sign a treaty of mutual co-operation known as the Pact of Steel.

Tuesday 23: The American submarine USS *Squalus* sinks during trials; a rescue operation successfully evacuates 33 crew members, but the remaining 26 are drowned.

Wednesday 24: Chinese troops defeat the Japanese at the Battle of Suixian-Zaoyang.

Thursday 25: Actor Sir Ian McKellen (*Lord of the Rings*) is born in Burnley, Lancashire.

Friday 26: Rescue attempts in the *Squalus* disaster are called off. She is later raised and refurbished as the USS *Sailfish* and engages in multiple actions in the Second World War.

Sir Ian McKellen, born 25 May.

Saturday 27: The ocean liner MS *St Louis*, carrying 900 German Jewish refugees, docks at Havana, Cuba; only 22 persons are allowed to disembark.

Sunday 28: In Hungarian elections, the fascist Arrow Cross party makes large gains and becomes the second largest party in parliament.

May/June 1939

Monday 29: Lt Gen Sir John Martin Carruthers Garrod OBE, former Commandant General of the Royal Marines, is born in Darjeeling, India. (Died 2009).

Tuesday 30: Essex defeats Worcestershire by 295 runs at Chelmsford on the last day of the cricket County Championship.

Wednesday 31: Celebrations are held in Hamburg in honour of 5,000 German troops returning from action in the Spanish Civil War.

Thursday 1: Just days after the USS *Squalus* disaster, the Royal Navy's submarine HMS *Thetis* sinks off the English coast near Liverpool with a loss of 99 lives; only four men are saved.

Friday 2: The Norwegian cargo ship *Besholt* catches fire at Philadelphia, Pennsylvania, causing severe damage.

Saturday 3: A treaty is signed in Rome giving Italy control over Albania's foreign affairs.

Sunday 4: The US Federal Communications Commission issues rules for radio stations broadcasting to other countries; they are to 'promote international goodwill, understanding and co-operation'.

Memorial in Birkenhead Priory to those who died on HMS *Thetis*.

June 1939

The King and Queen with President and Mrs Roosevelt on the USS *Potomac*, en route from Washington DC to Mount Vernon, VA.

Monday 5: Novelist Dame Margaret Drabble, Lady Holroyd, is born in Sheffield, England.

Tuesday 6: The first baseball match in the Little League for children is played at Williamsport, Pennsylvania.

Wednesday 7: TM King George VI and Queen Elizabeth cross from Canada into the USA at Niagra Falls. The King is the first reigning British sovereign to visit the United States.

Thursday 8: The King and Queen dine with President Roosevelt at the White House.

Friday 9: 20 letter bombs explode in post boxes across Britain as part of the IRA's terror campaign.

Saturday 10: An estimated two million people turn out to watch the Royal visit to New York City and the New York World's Fair.

Sunday 11: Racing driver Sir Jackie Stewart is born in Milton, West Dunbartonshire, Scotland.

June 1939

Monday 12: A painting by Watteau, *L'Indifferent*, is stolen in broad daylight from the Louvre in Paris. It is recovered two months later.

Tuesday 13: An international committee agrees to place the remaining German Jewish refugees on the MS *St Louis* in Belgium, the Netherlands, France and Britain.

Wednesday 14: A major diplomatic dispute, the Tientsen Incident takes place when occupying Japanese troops blockade British settlements in Tientsen, China; the dispute ends in a compromise as war between Britain and Japan is narrowly avoided.

Thursday 15: The Royal tour of North America ends as the King and Queen depart from Halifax, Nova Scotia.

Friday 16: US jazz band leader Chick Webb dies aged 34.

Saturday 17: The last public guillotining takes place in France as serial killer Eugen Weidmann is executed.

Sunday 18: 10 people are killed when a tornado hits Minnesota.

Japanese barricades erected around the British settlement at Tientsen, China.

June 1939

Central Haifa, 1939.

Monday 19: 18 arabs are killed when a bomb explodes in Haifa, British Mandatory Palestine (now Israel).

Tuesday 20: Ethnic Germans in Danzig (Gdansk) form their own SS unit.

Wednesday 21: Strict controls on the financial and business transactions of Jews are decreed in Bohemia and Moravia.

Thursday 22: TM King George VI and Queen Elizabeth return from their tour of North America.

Friday 23: France and Turkey sign a mutual assistance pact; France renounces claims to the Republic of Hatay situated between Turkey and French-controlled Syria.

Saturday 24: 20 people are injured as bombs explode in London's theatre district, thought to be planted as part of the IRA's mainland terror campaign.

Sunday 25: British racing driver Richard Seaman is killed, aged 26, when his car crashes in the Belgian Grand Prix.

June/July 1939

Monday 26: British writer Ford Madox Ford (*The Good Soldier, Parade's End*) dies aged 65.

Tuesday 27: French Prime Minister Édouard Daladier cuts short parliament's summer holiday due to the increase in German troop manoeuvres on the French border.

Wednesday 28: The Women's Auxiliary Air Force is created in the United Kingdom.

Thursday 29: Poland officially warns Germany that it will fight to defend Danzig from German takeover.

Friday 30: The Federal Theater Project, a programme of arts subsidies as part of Roosevelt's New Deal, comes to an end after Congress objects to the left-wing nature of some of its sponsored performances.

Saturday 1: The Irish Red Cross is formally established by nurse Elizabeth O'Herrin of Dublin City Hospital.

Sunday 2: The first World Science Fiction convention is held as part of the New York World's Fair.

From top: Édouard Daladier, Ford Madox Ford, WAAF recruitment poster.

July 1939

Monday 3: British Prime Minister Neville Chamberlain warns Parliament about 'intensive measures of a military character' taking place in Danzig.

Tuesday 4: The *Daily Telegraph* begins a campaign to have Winston Churchill MP given a place in the British Cabinet.

Wednesday 5: Chinese troops force the Japanese to retreat over the Khalkhyn River.

Thursday 6: The McDonnell aircraft manufacturing company is founded in St Louis, Missouri.

Friday 7: Bobby Riggs defeats fellow American Elwood Cooke in the men's tennis final at Wimbledon.

Saturday 8: Medical author and sexologist Havelock Ellis, author of the first medical textbook on homosexuality, dies aged 80.

Sunday 9: Mass rallies are held in Danzig by the German population who demand Hitler takes over the city.

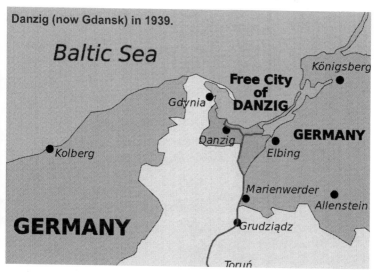

Danzig (now Gdansk) in 1939.

July 1939

Monday 10: Len Harvey defeats Jock McAvoy in the British Light Heavyweight boxing championships held at White City, London.

Tuesday 11: The US Foreign Relations Committee defeats President Roosevelt's attempts to move the USA to a less isolationist position.

Wednesday 12: Italy recalls its ambassador from London.

Thursday 13: The film *The Man in the Iron Mask* starring Louis Hayward and Joan Bennett is released.

Friday 14: Hundreds of British troops join French soldiers in Paris for Bastille Day celebrations, the first Anglo-French military parade since the Great War.

Joan Bennett.

Saturday 15: *Stairway to the Stars* by Glenn Miller reaches number one in the US charts compiled by radio show *Your Hit Parade.*

Sunday 16: British fascist leader Oswald Mosley addresses a crowd of 20,000 people at London's Earl's Court Exhibition Centre, and calls for the British Empire to avoid interfering in European affairs.

Oswald Mosley.

July 1939

Monday 17: Following threats from Japanese forces in China, British Prime Minister Neville Chamberlain refuses to change his country's policy in the far east.

Tuesday 18: President Roosevelt makes a further unsuccessful attempt to reverse the USA's neutrality policy. The 1935 Neutrality Act and subsequent updates forbid the USA from selling arms or war materials to foreign powers during time of war.

Wednesday 19: A group of RAF bombers make a test flight from London to Marseille. Commentators note the distance is roughly the same as that of London to Berlin.

Thursday 20: Benito Mussolini announces a plan to modernise and resettle Sicily with large-scale public works.

Friday 21: US diplomat and Deputy Secretary of State John Negroponte is born in London, England.

Mussolini.

Saturday 22: Seven weeks after its sinking, the Royal Navy submarine HMS *Thetis* is raised.

Sunday 23: Mahatma Gandhi writes to Adolf Hitler, addressing him as 'friend' and imploring him not to drag Europe into war. Hitler makes no official reply.

Former US Deputy Secretary of State John Negroponte, born 21 July.

July 1939

Monday 24: British Prime Minister Neville Chamberlain announces to Parliament that an agreement has been reached with Japan over the treatment of British citizens in occupied China; critics suggest Britain has sided with Japan against China.

Tuesday 25: The first Girl Guide and Girl Scout international jamboree is held at Gödöllő, Hungary.

Wednesday 26: One person is killed and 20 injured as IRA bombs explode in London and Liverpool.

Thursday 27: 40 addresses are raided in London in the hunt for IRA terrorists following the previous day's explosions.

Friday 28: Britain begins summary deportation of 19 IRA suspects.

Saturday 29: The French government orders the postponement of the country's general election for two years.

Sunday 30: Sylvère Maes of Belgium wins the Tour de France. It is the last Tour held until 1947.

Girl Guides and Girl Scouts at their first international Jamboree, held in Gödöllő, Hungary.

July/August 1939

Monday 31: Britain and France announce that talks will be held with a view to forming a pact with the Soviet Union.

Tuesday 1: Glenn Miller and his Orchestra record *In The Mood*. The tune tops the US charts for 13 weeks in 1940 and becomes one of the most popular big-band hits of all time.

Wednesday 2: Albert Einstein warns President Roosevelt in a letter that Nazi Germany could develop a nuclear bomb, and that in response, the USA should begin its own atomic weapons programme.

Thursday 3: Drummer Jimmie Nicol, the 'fifth Beatle' during Ringo Starr's illness on tour in 1964, is born in London, England.

Albert Einstein.

Jimmie Nicol, the 'fifth Beatle', born on 3 August.

Friday 4: A Chinese mob in Tientsin attacks the offices of the British International Export Corporation. The British claim the attack was instigated by the Japanese.

Saturday 5: The first flight of the regular Imperial Airways trans-Atlantic service leaves Southampton, England.

Sunday 6: Large crowds in Poland celebrate the twenty-fifth anniversary of its entry into the Great War.

August 1939

Monday 7: Swedish businessman Birger Dahlerus arranges a meeting in Schleswig-Holstein between his friend Hermann Göring and seven important British businessmen in an effort to avoid war.

Tuesday 8: 1300 warplanes fly across Britain in a series of air raid tests.

Wednesday 9: HM King George VI reviews the Royal Navy Reserve fleet at Weymouth.

Thursday 10: Citizens of the German protectorate of Bohemia and Moravia are ordered to hand in all firearms, on penalty of death.

Friday 11: A trial blackout of all lighting is held across England from midnight until four am to test air raid precautions.

Saturday 12: Actor George Hamilton is born in Memphis, Tennessee.

Sunday 13: 14 people are killed when a Pan-American Airways Sikorsky S43 passenger plane makes a crash landing at Rio de Janeiro, Brazil.

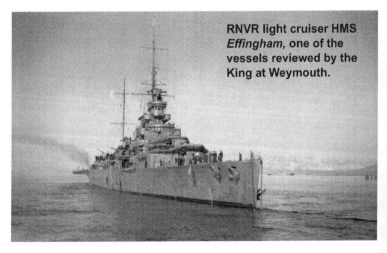

RNVR light cruiser HMS *Effingham*, one of the vessels reviewed by the King at Weymouth.

August 1939

Monday 14: US President Franklin Roosevelt announces that the Thanksgiving holiday will be moved from the last Thursday of November to the second-last, in order to give shops more time to sell Christmas merchandise.

Tuesday 15: *The Wizard of Oz*, starring Judy Garland, premieres at Grauman's Chinese Theatre in Hollywood.

Wednesday 16: A Polish soldier is shot dead without warning 20 yards inside the Danzig border. Polish forces are given orders to shoot any uniformed Germans on Polish territory.

Thursday 17: The German border with Poland in Upper Silesia is closed.

Sir Malcolm Campbell.

Friday 18: Germany begins its child euthanasia programme as doctors are given order to report children with severe mental or physical disability.

Saturday 19: Sir Malcolm Campbell sets the world water speed record in *Blue Bird K4* (141.740 mph/228.108 km/h) on Coniston Water, Lancashire, England.

Sunday 20: Germany and the USSR announce the German-Soviet credit agreement on trade.

August 1939

Monday 21: British and French attempts at forming a pact with the Soviet Union are called off after Poland refuses to allow the Red Army to pass through its territory.

Tuesday 22: The British parliament is recalled early from its summer recess for emergency war talks.

Wednesday 23: The Molotov-Ribbentrop pact is signed. Germany and the Soviet Union agree not to attack each other.

Thursday 24: The British parliament passes the Emergency Powers (Defence) Act 1939; Territorial Army reservists are called up and the Civil Defence Corps is mobilised.

Friday 25: Five people are killed when an IRA bomb explodes in Coventry, England.

Saturday 26: The first televised baseball game is broadcast in the USA on W2XBS as the Brooklyn Dodgers play the Cincinnati Reds at Ebbet's Field, Brooklyn, NY.

Sunday 27: Swedish diplomat Birgher Dahlerus begins shuttle diplomacy between Berlin and London, attempting to broker a compromise with a German annexation of Danzig.

IRA bomb damage in Coventry.

August/September 1939

Monday 28: The border between France and Germany is closed.

Tuesday 29: Adolf Hitler tells the British government that Germany must take control of Danzig and the Polish Corridor, but stresses the desire for 'lasting friendship' with Britain.

Wednesday 30: The Polish armed forces are mobilised.

Thursday 31: The Royal Navy is mobilised; British authorities order the evacuation of children from large cities and towns to the countryside.

Friday 1: The German invasion of Poland begins at 4.44 am when the battleship *Schleswig-Holstein* opens fire on a military base in Westerplatte. British Ambassador Sir Neville Henderson hands the German foreign minister Von Ribbentrop a final note demanding cessation of hostilities with Polish forces.

German troops remove a Polish border post.

Saturday 2: The government of Éire (Southern Ireland) declares its neutrality and declares a State of Emergency.

Sunday 3: At 11.15am Britain's Prime Minister Neville Chamberlain announces on the radio that all attempts at diplomacy with Germany have failed, and that Britain is at war with Germany. The King makes a special broadcast at 6.00pm.

September 1939

Monday 4: Winston Churchill is appointed First Lord of the Admiralty. RAF bombers attack German ships at Wilhelmshaven and Brunsbüttel.

Tuesday 5: The USA officially declares its neutrality.

Wednesday 6: German troops take Krakow in southern Poland.

Thursday 7: French forces engage the German army in the Saarland Offensive.

Children in besieged Warsaw.

Friday 8: The Siege of Warsaw begins as German troops attack the city.

Saturday 9: Glenn Miller and Ray Eberle's version of *Over the Rainbow* tops the American music charts.

Sunday 10: Canada declares war on Germany. A special edition of the *Canada Gazette* publishes the declaration by the Governor General, Lord Tweedsmuir.

September 1939

Monday 11: German troops are held back at the Battle of Jaroslaw in Poland, enabling Polish cavalry to mobilise.

Tuesday 12: The Duke of Windsor, Britain's former King Edward VIII, returns to England from Paris with his wife the Duchess of Windsor.

Wednesday 13: The Battle of Modlin begins in Poland.

Thursday 14: The German submarine U-39 becomes the first U-boat to be sunk in the war, after an unsuccesful attack on HMS *Ark Royal* at Rockall Bank.

Friday 15: Aeronaut Charles Lindbergh makes a nationwide radio broadcast in the USA in support of American neutrality, saying 'We must either keep out of European wars entirely or stay in European affairs permanently'.

Saturday 16: French troops withdraw after the failure of the Saar Offensive against Germany.

Sunday 17: The Soviet Union invades Poland from the east.

Soviet troops in Poland.

September 1939

Monday 18: Britain's William Joyce, known as 'Lord Haw-Haw', begins making pro-Nazi broadcasts from Germany. He is executed for treason in 1945.

Hitler's victorious entry into Danzig.

Tuesday 19: Hitler enters the conquered city of Danzig, and makes a speech denouncing the Polish government.

Wednesday 20: Joe Louis retains the World Heavyweight title, knocking out Bob Pastor in the eleventh round at Briggs Stadium in Detroit.

Thursday 21: US President Roosevelt asks Congress to amend the Neutrality Acts to allow countries fighting Germany to purchase American weapons.

Friday 22: Polish troops surrender the city of Lwow to the Germans.

Saturday 23: Psychoanalyst Sigmund Freud dies in London aged 83.

Sunday 24: The Luftwaffe bombs the Polish capital, Warsaw, causing widespread destruction.

Sigmund Freud.

September/October 1939

Monday 25: A tropical cyclone hits San Pedro, California, the only tropical cyclone to do so in the twentieth century.

Tuesday 26: The British score their first hit against a German aircraft, as the Fleet Air Arm shoot down a Dornier DO8 over Dogger Bank in the North Sea.

Wednesday 27: Britain's Chancellor of the Exchequer Sir John Simon introduces an emergency war budget, raising income tax and duties on alcohol, sugar and tobacco.

Thursday 28: The Siege of Warsaw ends after 20 days as Polish forces capitulate to the Germans.

Friday 29: Major clashes occur between Polish and Soviet troops at Parczew, Jabłoń and Milanów.

Saturday 30: As the situation in Poland deteriorates, a Polish Government-in-Exile is established in Paris.

General Tadeusz Kutrzeba, CO of the Polish forces in Warsaw, surrenders.

German colours are raised at Westerplatte garrison, Poland.

Sunday 1: Winston Churchill addresses the British nation on the state of the war, and famously describes Russia as 'a riddle wrapped in a mystery inside an enigma.'

October 1939

Monday 2: After facing overwhelming odds for several weeks, a small pocket of Polish resistance surrenders to German troops in the Hel Peninsula.

Tuesday 3: The Panama Conference ends with a general declaration of neutrality by the Latin American republics and a ban on combatant submarines entering their ports.

Wednesday 4: Adolf Hitler issues a secret amnesty for all crimes committed by German military and police in Poland between 1 September and 4 October.

Thursday 5: The Battle of Kock ends with a Soviet and German victory over Poland. Polish forces carry on fighting against occupation with underground resistance.

Friday 6: Author and broadcaster Melyvn Bragg is born in Carlisle, Cumbria.

Saturday 7: The British Expeditionary Force arrives in France.

Paul Hogan.

Sunday 8: Actor Paul Hogan (*Crocodille Dundee*) is born in Lightning Ridge, New South Wales, Australia.

A French girl gives flowers to British soldiers newly arrived in France.

October 1939

Monday 9: The American freighter SS *City of Flint* is captured by the crew of the German cruiser *Deutschland* in the north Atlantic.

Tuesday 10: France's Prime Minister, Édouard Daladier, goes on air to reject Germany's peace proposals as untrustworthy.

Wednesday 11: Actor Jackie Coogan (*The Kid*) divorces starlet Betty Grable *(right)* after two years of marriage.

Thursday 12: British Prime Minister Neville Chamberlain rejects Hitler's peace proposals, stating 'Past experience has shown that no reliance can be placed upon the promises of the present German Government.'

Friday 13: German submarines U-40 and U-42 are sunk off the British coast.

HMS *Royal Oak.*

Saturday 14: 883 men are killed as the German submarine U-47 attacks the British naval base at Scapa Flow in Scotland, and sinks HMS *Royal Oak.*

Sunday 15: A crowd of almost 100,000 gather to watch the inauguration of New York's Municipal Airport (later named La Guardia Airport). It is the first airport for New York City, which up to this point has been served by the airport at Newark, NJ.

October 1939

Monday 16: The comedy play *The Man Who Came to Dinner* by George S. Kaufman and Moss Hart premieres on Broadway.

Tuesday 17: The first German bomb is dropped on the United Kingdom, at Hoy in the Orkney Islands.

Wednesday 18: Lee Harvey Oswald, assassin of President John F. Kennedy, is born in New Orleans, Louisiana. (Killed in 1963).

The Marx Brothers.

Thursday 19: The Anglo-French-Turkish Treaty of Mutual Assistance is signed in Ankara.

Friday 20: The Marx Brothers Metro-Goldwyn-Mayer comedy film *At the Circus* is released, in which Groucho Marx sings *Lydia the Tattooed Lady.*

Saturday 21: Registration of British men aged 20-23 for military conscription (the 'call up') begins.

Sunday 22: American football is televised for the first time as NBC broadcasts a game between the Philadelphia Eagles and the Brooklyn Dodgers to approximately 500 sets in the New York area, and to crowds in the New York World's Fair.

October 1939

Monday 23: The prolific American western author Zane Grey (*Riders of the Purple Sage*) dies aged 67.

Tuesday 24: German foreign minister Joachim von Ribbentrop blames Britain for the war as it had refused Hitler's offer of peace, and states that fighting will now intensify.

Polish Jews forced to wear Star of David.

Wednesday 25: Jews in Poland are ordered to wear the yellow star on their clothing.

Thursday 26: Jews in Poland aged 14-60 are ordered to undertake forced labour.

Friday 27: Actor John

John Cleese.

Cleese (*Monty Python, Fawlty Towers, A Fish Called Wanda*) is born in Weston-super-Mare, England.

Saturday 28: Mass protests against German occupation of Czechoslovakia.

Sunday 29: Soviet troops occupy Latvia.

October/November 1939

Monday 30: Winston Churchill is narrowly saved from death whilst on the battleship HMS *Nelson* off Orkney; the German submarine U-56 fires three torpedoes at the vessel, none of which explode.

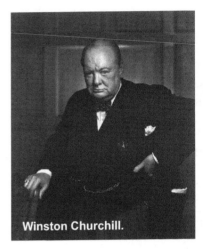

Winston Churchill.

Tuesday 31: The Soviet Union gives an ultimatum to Finland, demanding use of the city of Hanko as a naval base.

Wednesday 1: Martial law is declared in the Netherlands along the German border.

Thursday 2: The Polish Government-in-Exile dissolves Parliament and sets up a National Council in its place.

Friday 3: The USA amends the 1937 Neutrality Act, allowing arms to be sold to foreign combatant nations.

Saturday 4: After docking in neutral Norway, the USS *City of Flint*, captured by Germans on 9 October, is seized and its illegal crew are interned. The ship is restored to US control.

Sunday 5: Three German Army commanders (Fedor von Bock, Wilhelm Ritter von Leeb and Gerd von Rundstedt) hold a secret meeting to discuss ways of dissuading Hitler from an attack on France.

Fedor von Bock.

November 1939

Monday 6: 183 professors of Jagiellonian University in Kraków are arrested by occupying German forces; 163 are sent to Sachsenhausen concentration camp.

Tuesday 7: The Polish government-in-exile appoints Władysław Sikorski as head of its armed forces.

Sikorski.

Wednesday 8: Eight people are killed in Munich in a failed assassination attempt on Adolf Hitler by anti-Nazi Johann Elser.

Thursday 9: Supreme allied commander Maurice Gamelin reveals his Dyle Plan for the defence of France.

Friday 10: The United States Circuit Court of Appeal in Philadelphia rules that it is unconstitutional to force school pupils to salute the US flag if it is against their religious beliefs.

Saturday 11: No official Armistice Day ceremony takes place at the Cenotaph in London's Whitehall, although unofficial observations occur across the country.

Sunday 12: German authorities begin the deportation of Jews from Polish territories.

Hitler salutes the victims of the failed assassination attempt in Munich.

November 1939

Monday 13: HMS *Blanche* is sunk by a mine in the Thames Estuary, the first destroyer lost to enemy action in the war.

Tuesday 14: The Great Synagogue of Lodz in Poland is completely destroyed in a German arson attack.

Wednesday 15: The Battle of South Guangxi begins in the Sino-Japanese War.

Thursday 16: Gangster Al Capone is released from federal custody on health grounds after serving seven and a half years for tax evasion.

Friday 17: Thousands of students are arrested in the former Czechoslovakia by German occupying forces; nine Czechs are executed without trial for their alleged role in recent anti-German demonstrations.

Saturday 18: Novelist Margaret Atwood (*The Handmaid's Tale*) is born in Ottawa, Canada.

Sunday 19: Baseball star Joe DiMaggio marries actress Dorothy Arnold in North Beach, San Francisco.

The Great Synagogue of Lodz.

November 1939

Monday 20: DC Comics publishes *Flash Comics* #1 featuring the first appearance of superheroes Flash and Hawkman. They go on to become extremely popular characters still in print to the present day.

Tuesday 21: Britain announces a naval blockade of all German exports. Prime Minister Neville Chamberlain blames the decision on 'the many violations of international law and the ruthless brutality of German methods'.

Wednesday 22: The US Supreme Court decides in Schneider *v.* State of New Jersey that municipal legislation against distributing handbills in the street is a violation of free speech.

Thursday 23: The British armed merchantman HMS *Rawlpindi* is sunk by German warships north of the Faroe Islands; 238 are killed including its captain, Edward Coverly Kennedy, father of TV broadcaster Ludovic Kennedy.

Tina Turner.

Friday 24: Imperial Airways and British Airways Ltd. merge to form British Overseas Airways Corporation (BOAC). The corporation merges with British European Airways (BEA) in 1974 and receives its current name, British Airways.

Saturday 25: After already having to move the 1940 Winter Olympics venue from Japan to Germany due to the Sino-Japanese war, the International Olympic Committee announces the complete cancellation of the relocated Games.

Sunday 26: Singer Tina Turner (*What's Love Got To Do With It, Simply The Best*) is born in Nutbush, Tennessee.

November/December 1939

Finnish troops combat the Soviets in the Winter War.

Monday 27: Maxwell Anderson's play *Key Largo* opens on Broadway; it is later made into a film starring Humphrey Bogart and Lauren Bacall.

Tuesday 28: Following its exhibition at the New York World's Fair, His Majesty's Government ceremonially presents the US government with its copy of the Magna Carta for safekeeping for the duration of the war.

Wednesday 29: Hitler announces that British ports will be blockaded and its shipping attacked.

Thursday 30: The 'Winter War' begins as the Soviet Union invades Finland.

Friday 1: The Soviet Union creates the puppet state of the Finnish Democratic Republic.

Saturday 2: The Roosevelt Administration in the USA imposes a 'moral embargo' on the Soviet Union, urging American companies not to sell to them.

Sunday 3: Princess Louise, the sixth child of Queen Victoria, dies aged 91.

December 1939

Monday 4: The German submarine U-36 is sunk in the Heligoland Bight by the British submarine *Salmon*.

Tuesday 5: Soviet troops reach the Mannerheim Line defences in southern Finland.

Wednesday 6: The musical *DuBarry Was a Lady* with music by Cole Porter opens at the 46th Street Theatre on Broadway.

Thursday 7: The German SS begins a euthanasia programme on patients at the Dziekanka Psychiatric Hospital in Gniezno, Poland; a total of 1043 people are killed.

Friday 8: Flautist James Galway OBE is born in Belfast, Northern Ireland.

Saturday 9: Corporal Thomas Priday becomes the first soldier of the British Expeditionary Force to be killed after triggering a French landmine.

Sunday 10: The 1939 Nobel Prizes are awarded in Stockholm. The recipients are Ernest Lawrence of the United States for Physics, Adolf Butenandt (Germany) and Leopold Ružička (Switzerland) for Chemistry, Gerhard Domagk (Germany) for Physiology or Medicine and Frans Eemil Sillanpää of Finland for Literature. The Peace Prize is not awarded.

Soviet troops reach the heavily defended Mannerheim Line in Finland.

December 1939

Monday 11: The League of Nations calls for the Soviet Union to cease hostilities with Finland.

Tuesday 12: Hollywood actor Douglas Fairbanks (*The Mark Of Zorro*) dies aged 56.

Wednesday 13: The Battle of the River Plate: the German cruiser Admiral Graf Spee is crippled in a battle with the British warships Exeter, Ajax and Achilles in south American waters.

Clark Gable and Vivien Leigh in *Gone With The Wind*.

Thursday 14: The League of Nations expels the Soviet Union over its military action in Finland, leaving only Britain and France as members.

Friday 15: The epic romance film *Gone with the Wind* starring Vivien Leigh and Clark Gable premieres at Loew's Grand Theatre in Atlanta, Georgia.

Saturday 16: In Finland, the First Battle of Summa in the Winter War with the Soviet Union begins.

Sunday 17: The German cruiser Graf Spee is scuttled in neutral waters off Montevideo, Uruaguay by the captain, Hans Langdorff, who believes that British ships are nearby and the ship will not be able to fight with limited supplies of ammunition.

December 1939

Monday 18: The Battle of Heligoland Bight begins between British and German air forces over northern Germany.

Tuesday 19: English composer Eric Fogg dies aged 39.

Wednesday 20: A fundraiser for the Finnish Relief Fund takes place in New York's Madison Square Garden with former US President Herbert Hoover.

Thursday 21: Soviet forces temporarily halt fighting in Finland as they re-group in the face of stiff resistance.

Friday 22: The First Battle of Summa ends in a Finnish victory.

Saturday 23: Dutch aviation pioneer Anthony Fokker dies aged 49.

Sunday 24: Pope Pius XII gives a Christmas address to 25 cardinals outlining plans for negotiating a 'just and honourable peace'.

Pilots of 452 Squadron RAAF, the first Australian unit in the UK.

December 1939

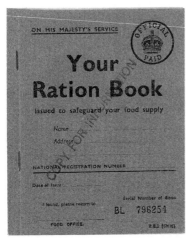

Child's ration coupons book issued by Britain's Ministry of Food.

Monday 25: The Battle of Kelja begins in Finland.

Tuesday 26: The first Australian airmen arrive in Britain.

Wednesday 27: Over 32,000 people are killed when an earthquake hits Erzincan in eastern Turkey.

Thursday 28: Britain's Minister for Food, W.S. Morrison, announces that food rationing will begin on 8 January.

Friday 29: *The Hunchback of Notre Dame* starring Charles Laughton and Maureen O'Hara is released.

Saturday 30: German air chief Hermann Göring announces that when the Luftwaffe attack Britain 'it will make an assault such as world history never has experienced.'

Sunday 31: New Year's Eve observances in Britain, France and Germany are subdued with very few public celebrations. German propaganda minister Joseph Goebbels in a radio address predicts that 1940 will be 'a hard year, and we must be ready for it'.

Maureen O'Hara as Esmerelda in *The Hunchback of Notre Dame*.

Birthday Notebooks
...a great alternative to a card.

Handy 60 page ruled notebooks with a significant event from the year heading each page.

Available from Montpelier Publishing at Amazon.

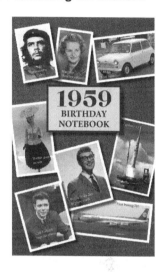

Made in the USA
Coppell, TX
16 November 2019

11252119R00033